SLA | GUIDE

Budgeting for Success

Planning and Managing the Primary School Library Finances

Karen Horsfield
and Susan Staniforth

Series Editor: Geoff Dubber

School Library Association

Acknowledgements

This book updates the SLA Guideline *Making Ends Meet* published in 2010. The authors would like to acknowledge the help and support of Sally Duncan, Geoff Dubber and Jayne Gould who advised on the initial edition of this publication, also Richard Leveridge and Jane Cooper, key members of the SLA's excellent Publications Team. Karen Horsfield and Geoff Dubber would like to thank our good SLA friend and colleague, Susan Staniforth, for updating this publication for us.

Series Editor's note: For the purposes of this publication the terms School/Library Development Plan, School Library Improvement Plan are interchangeable, so too School Management Team (SMT) and School Leadership Team (SLT).

 School Libraries must have adequate and sustained funding for trained staff, materials, technologies and facilities. They must be free of charge.

— Extract from the School Library Manifesto.
UNESCO/IFLA not dated.
http://www.unesco.org/webworld/libraries/
manifestos/school_manifesto.html

Published by

School Library Association
1 Pine Court, Kembrey Park
Swindon SN2 8AD

Tel: 01793 530166   Fax: 01793 481182
E-mail: info@sla.org.uk
Web: www.sla.org.uk

Registered Charity No: 313660
Charity Registered in Scotland No: SC039453

Second Edition
© School Library Association 2017. All rights reserved.
ISBN: 978-1-911222-08-8

Cover photographs by Richard Leveridge
Printed by Holywell Press, Oxford

Contents

Introduction

'Around the school an attractive and well-stocked library is often an indicator of effective support for pupils' wider reading and information retrieval' (Ofsted 2011[1]) ... yet there is no statutory requirement for schools in England to have one.

Research (*School Libraries: A Plan for Improvement,* 2010) shows that there is a clear link between the quality of a school's library and the general well being of the pupils and their literacy levels and there are other cross curricular benefits.[2] The library should be the heart of the school supporting all the pupils and staff. There is a huge variation in the type of libraries that exist in primary schools, ranging from two large book cases in the main corridor to separate Key Stage One and Key Stage Two libraries (*School Libraries in 2012* – SLA survey[3]). Some primary schools provide a real reading culture with an exciting range of attractive books in a well-stocked, effectively managed and well-used library. They have a vision and they find the budget. Unsurprisingly in other schools library use and funding are moot points; not all primary schools allocate a specific figure for the library budget so that books and other library resources may appear under various financial headings and in any case budgets are generally declining according to the School Libraries in the UK report in 2010. Since that date anecdotal evidence from schools supports this trend of a continuing decline. Each department and every class needs money and to simply state that the library needs lots of cash too is not enough! According to the All Party Parliamentary Group report in 2014, 40% of primary schools with designated library space had seen their budgets reduced which confirms the figures that were produced four years earlier. In order to compete for funding it is essential to do the following:

- plan
- collect data
- create documentation to support your budget requests
- communicate regularly with those who are responsible for the overall budget in the school.

These activities are the responsibility of the library coordinator and this guideline will explain how you can go about achieving these things.

The Chartered Institute of Library and Information Professionals (CILIP) recommends ten to thirteen books for every pupil of primary age excluding textbooks, structured readers and class sets.[4]

The School Library Association (SLA) recommends that smaller schools need proportionately more items per pupil, so that schools with fewer than 100 pupils should aim for a minimum base figure of 1,300 quality library books. These figures presuppose that not only the school library budget will stretch to provide these numbers of books but that the library will be sufficiently

---

[1] See the full report Reading, Writing, Communication (Ofsted, 2011) at
    http://dera.ioe.ac.uk/12273/2/Reading,_writing_and_communication_(literacy)%5B1%5D.pdf

[2] http://www.literacytrust.org.uk/assets/0000/5718/School_Libraries_A_Plan_for_Improvement.pdf

[3] http://www.sla.org.uk/sla-survey-2012.php

[4] http://primaryschoollibraryguidelines.org.uk/policyAndPlanning/budgets

large to accommodate them all. There are many primary schools where space is at a premium and the library is housed in a space that is not really adequate. The SLA also proposes that the school library can only be an effective provider of resources if sufficient funding is available to allow managed development of the provision. If the library is to be attractive and relevant there should be enough funding for at least ten per cent of the library book stock to be replaced each year though not necessarily like for like with additional funding to bring resources up to a suitable level. Staff will also need to consider its current and future ICT provision too.

'There is a direct link between well-funded libraries and effectiveness.'[5]

The Primary School Library Guidelines (CILIP, SLA, ASCEL 2016) echoes this message by stating

There are three elements to a successful library:

- people to run it
- books and resources to put in it
- space to accommodate it.

They go on further to recommend that an effective library should:

- Create a whole school culture that values reading, with the library as a pivot
- Have a librarian/staff member who works in the library regularly
- **Allocate a budget for the library so there are finances to provide a wide range of new resources**
- Make the library welcoming – rugs, soft seating, a warm atmosphere and displays all help
- Keep the library as a library, not as storage space or a group work space
- Make sure all school staff have knowledge of how the library works so that they can support pupils when they choose books, and encourage reading for pleasure
- Use a computerised library management system for pupils for issuing, teaching information skills, tracking reading (see Library Management Systems)
- Create library helpers to keep the library tidy and to help other pupils choose a book to read (see Pupil librarians)
- Run interactive activities in the library, with quizzes, competitions, book weeks and more
- Give pupils regular times to visit the library, e.g. with their class, at lunchtime, after school and allow time for browsing when pupils come into the library – do not rush them.

Ofsted concludes that even the best-funded libraries struggle to meet the levels recommended by CILIP.

'There is marked variability in funding for libraries, even across schools with good libraries – even the best-funded school libraries struggled to meet the most commonly recommended levels of funding.'[6]

---

[5] OFSTED. Good School Libraries 2006 p8

[6] OFSTED op cit.

In CILIP's response (December 2014) to Ofsted's consultation document *Better Inspection For All* [7] they state that a well-managed and resourced library underpins and enriches the curriculum, supporting both teaching and learning. They went on further to state that there is a positive correlation between a good school library and student attainment, achievement and motivation and that a school library programme that is sufficiently staffed, resourced and funded can lead to higher student achievement regardless of the socio-economic or educational levels of a community.

England's Department for Education through its National Curriculum for primary schools states that:

- every school to provide a library facility
- all pupils must be encouraged to read widely and often for both pleasure and information
- pupils should learn to retrieve and record information from non-fiction and they should be shown how to use contents pages and indexes to location information.

While this is welcome, provision currently varies from excellent to invisible, with many head teachers perceiving the library as low priority.

Technology is no longer an option for the primary school library and it needs to complement the book stock. This presents a wonderful opportunity for the library to become integral to the curriculum – I cannot think of a better place for children to become independent and confident users of information. Technology now forms a vital part of the curriculum and who better than the librarian/library coordinator to exploit technology to enrich learning across the curriculum? However, you will need a budget in order to do this!

Schools are increasingly being asked to spread their budget further and further and although primary school departments/subject areas may be allocated a basic budget they may be asked to bid for additional funding.

This guideline aims to help the primary school library coordinator and staff in the primary school library to:

- Understand the definition of a budget
- Consider budget plans
- Make budget requests
- Consider how to utilise the library budget
- Help in budget presentation in order to communicate your ideas for library spending.

Obtaining and managing the budget is one of the key tasks for all primary school library coordinators.

---

[7] *Better Inspection for All: CILIP's Response* [pdf]
http://www.cilip.org.uk/sites/default/files/documents/Better%20inspection%20for%20all%20-%20CILIP%20response%20Dec%202014_0.pdf

Why Budget?

The SLA believes that the school library should be adequately funded on an annual basis in line with other school budget areas and that these figures should be published to parents.[8]

By creating a budget or a financial plan you will be able to:

- Define how much it will cost to achieve the aims and objectives of your library, both during this current year and with regard to its development plan for future years

- Allocate those funds so that they are spent wisely throughout the year and there is no over or under spend which could result in a budget cut

- Safeguard funds and make effective use of them by ensuring that basic needs are met and providing an effective brake on impulse spending

- Account for the way that the funding has been spent to the Head Teacher, Governing Body, SMT, Inspectors, Bursar/Finance Manager, parents and even explaining to a pupil why you won't be buying that very expensive book s/he has asked for!

- Track the funding and ensure that it is being used properly

- Evaluate the use of the funds

- Predict how to meet the future needs of the library

- Attract further funding

- Give you peace of mind that the money has been accounted for.

Of course, a well-managed budget will also give a professional image to the library and help raise its profile amongst stakeholders.

Comparisons

So – what are other people getting?

Booktrust has recommended that £10 per pupil per academic year be spent in primary schools but 61% of schools reported a total library spend well below this figure. Research commissioned by them (2007 was the last year this was commissioned) in 255 state primary schools in each of the nine English regions provides approximate library budgets by school size.[9] The findings are displayed in the Table in Appendix 2.

The research indicated that there was great diversity in budget allocation between primary school libraries and resource provision. Some very large primary schools spent very little on their library while smaller ones had a comparatively generous budget.

The average library budget a decade ago was £2,682 for the Booktrust schools.[10]

---

[8] http://www.sla.org.uk/primary-charter.php

[9] Book Trust: *Library Books in Schools. Spending and Provision in Primary and Secondary Schools in England.* 2007.
http://booktrustadmin.kentlyons.com/downloads/publicfinance.pdf

[10] op cit.

The SLA conducted a new survey of school libraries in 2012, which showed that the majority of budgets for primary schools are under £1,000 with 41% of the total being under £500. The responses to the question 'What is your library budget?' are shown in the graph below.[11]

Ofsted (2013) concluded that:

> 'Where librarians are fully integrated into the management structure of the school, they have the opportunity to influence debate and to enhance the library's contribution to pupils' progress.' [12]

Your local Schools' Library Service may be able to advise about funding of other local primary school libraries in order that you can benchmark the funding that you receive. What resources and services do they provide and how do these compare to your own?

Survey of Primary School Library Budgets

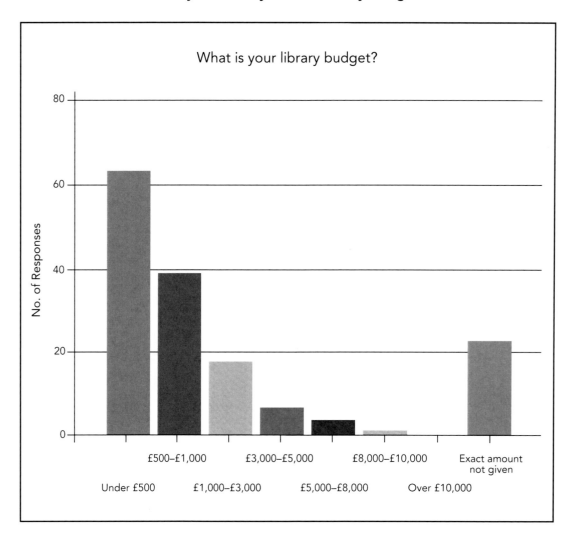

---

[11] http://www.sla.org.uk/sla-survey-2012.php

[12] https://www.gov.uk/government/uploads/system/uploads/attachment_data/file/413182/Improving_literacy_in_secondary_schools.pdf (accessed 4 October 2016)

What is Available?

There isn't a right or wrong way to manage the school library budget. It depends on individual school policies and personalities, but here are some key points to reflect upon.

- The managers of your school will only have access to a finite sum of money, which they will use to meet its targets. If the library is not seen as a priority it is bound to dip out. Demonstrate that the library is key to supporting teaching and learning and you will be halfway to receiving some reasonable funding. **School libraries that cannot demonstrate their worth tend to receive very little as nobody quite knows what they do and a spiral of neglect and decline can easily set in**.

- Discuss the allocation of funding with both your line manager and informally with colleagues to ascertain how the funds are divided. A lack of communication may mean that you could miss opportunities for funding.

- As library budget holder you must have a clear overview of the day to day budgetary requirements of the library, the process for obtaining funding and the in-house system for recording and monitoring financial activities.

- However, you must also have a clear view of where the library is going and how it will develop.

- If you are responsible for the library but do not have control of spending the library budget it is essential that you liaise with the person who is responsible for the funding and demonstrate a good case for continued or ideally enhanced library funding.

The School Library Association states in its *Primary School Library Charter*:

We believe that the school library should be adequately funded on an annual basis in line with other school budget areas and that these budget figures should be provided to parents.

—School Library Association, 2015. Available at
http://www.sla.org.uk/primary-charter

Budget Preparation

CILIP, SLA and ASCEL primary school library guideline in 2016 recommends:

- 10–13 quality library books for every pupil. This excludes textbooks, structured readers and class sets
- Smaller schools need proportionately more items per pupil, so schools with fewer than 100 pupils should aim for a minimum base figure of 1,300 quality library books
- Books wear out or become outdated and the average life expectancy of a book is 10 years (for some it is a lot less!) so schools should work on 10% replacement per annum, but not necessarily like for like
- The annual library budget should cover at least the cost of replacing 10% of library stock, with additional funding made available to bring resources up to a suitable level.

Some calculations useful for benchmarking:

- To calculate your library stock per pupil, divide the number of library books by the number of pupils
  - *Does your library stock meet the CILIP benchmark of 13 books per pupil?*
  - *Is the range balanced and appropriate for the needs of the pupils?*
- To calculate the stock renewal rate, divide the total library stock by the number of library books purchased last year + the number of books exchanged via SLS last year
  - *Effective use of the School Library Service exchange might assist your school to meet the 10% stock renewal recommendation of this service is offered locally*
- To calculate the minimum book fund needed to replace stock: divide the total stock by 10 and multiply by £10 *(this is the average cost of library books for primary age children).*

You can begin to prepare your budget in the Autumn Term if you are an LEA school with the financial year running from April to March but if you are an academy with funding running from August to July you will need to begin preparing your budget in the Spring Term. There should be two strands.

1. Maintenance of current resources and services.

2. Developing the library.

Prepare it well in advance so that it is ready to be submitted at the right time – and you need to find out when that is!

Remember to ascertain whether you have an SLS subscription and if so, whether it comes from this budget or from a separate school budget heading.

Taking Stock, Maintaining the Status Quo

Assuming that you need to bid for funding (perhaps for the first time) rather than simply agree a figure with the head teacher, you might want to bring the library up to scratch.

Step back and consider the function of the library in your particular school.

- Does it just house non-fiction and is the fiction kept in book corners in the classrooms?
- If the fiction is kept in book corners how are they funded? They should really be managed and budgeted for through the library.
- Is the fiction kept in the library or is there a combination of provision in your school?
- Is the library used for research during curriculum time?
- Is it open at break and lunchtimes times for the pupils to browse and to support reading for leisure and pleasure?
- Are pupils able to use the library before and after school?
- Is the library coordinator or person who runs the library on a day-to-day basis available for study support?

Whatever happens in your school, one thing remains the same – all activities, resources and services will need funding.

You may wish to extend the resources and services the library offers and we we'll address that later when we look at development planning.

The Current Situation

Funding should be provided with a purpose and therefore you need to consider the current situation and be clear about how much it will cost to bring the library up to recommended levels and then develop it further.

In order to prepare a case to be presented to management for next year's budget consider the funding required to keep it running at its current level. Here are some questions that you might like to ask yourself. The following **Funding Check Sheet** will help you to pull together a snapshot of your library.

Funding Check Sheet

How much central funding was received last year?	£
Current average book price? ❖	£
Current library spending per pupil?	£
Recommended spending level per pupil?	£
Number of pupils in the school?	_____
Number of books in the library?	_____
The ratio of books per pupil. We recommend that 13 – 18 books per pupil is provided by the school library. How does this compare with your ratio?	_____
The balance between fiction and non-fiction. We recommend a 50–50 balance	_____
Does the stock meet the teaching and learning requirements of the school community?	_____
Does the stock support reading for leisure and pleasure?	_____
Did your school's last Ofsted report comment on the library?	_____
How was the library's last budget total spent?	
▦ Fiction	£
▦ Non-fiction	£
▦ Picture books	£
▦ Book bags	£
▦ ICT – software/on-line resources	£
▦ CDs and DVDs – story and music and information	£
▦ Newspapers, magazines and comics	£
▦ Posters	£

❖ Average book price as given at SLA website:
www.sla.org.uk/advice-average-price.php (Members Only part of the website)

■ **Office supplies**	
■ Library stationery	£
■ Subscriptions e.g School Library Service	£
■ Repairs	£
■ Professional development	£
■ Furnishings and fittings	£
■ Events/promotions	£
■ Reprographic costs	£
■ ICT provision. Does any hardware need replacing?	£
■ Artefacts	£
■ Puppets and toys	£
■ Other	£
How much funding was received from:	
■ Governors	£
■ Sponsorship/donations	£
■ Parents	£
■ Other e.g. proceeds of book fair?	£
Number of books in poor condition and in need of replacing? Multiply by average book price❖ to create a total.	_____ £
How much stock is lost and needs replacing? Multiply by the average book price.❖	_____ £
Does the library subscribe to any publications either printed matter or electronic?	_____
How much stock needs to be purchased to bring the library up to the recommended stock level? Multiply by average book price.❖	_____ £

❖ Average book price as given at SLA website:
www.sla.org.uk/advice-average-price.php (Members Only part of the website)

How Was Last Year's Funding Gained?

■ Did you bid for last year's funding or was it simply allocated and accepted? Were your ideas for the library discussed?

■ Did you consult other members of the school community? Remember, the library is a whole school resource and asking other subject leaders to contribute is a perfect way of gaining funding.

■ Have the governors been consulted? Often Governors have access to all sorts of 'pots' of money. The right word in the right place could secure some of it for the library!

■ Did the Parent Teacher/Friends Association provide any funding? Although this is always a welcome addition, it should not be relied upon as a permanent source of funding. It is not logical, satisfactory or educational to use this as the major source of annual funding!

■ Did you receive any funding as a result of a bid to the Foyle Foundation?

The figures from the SLA's 2012 survey[13] or others known to you can be presented to the Head Teacher/SMT/Governors who will need to understand the importance of books and other library resources. Of course ICT has its place but it is important that you can explain how these figures have been reached and are able to stress the continued vital importance of children engaged in the information seeking process using books as well as IT resources with raising standards through reading for leisure and pleasure.

[13] http://www.sla.org.uk/sla-survey-2012.php

Developing the Library

The previous section discussed maintaining the status quo. It does not take into account further developments. It is very important that the library develops alongside the rest of the school and for this reason you need to consider the bigger picture.

The Library Development / Improvement Plan

Good libraries don't happen by chance. An action plan is needed, based on a whole school agenda. For more information about policy making and development planning see the SLA publication *Practical Paperwork: Policy Making and Development Planning for the Primary School Library* (SLA, 2007).

All schools have a development plan. This will consider the school's future needs and be revised and updated on an annual basis. Every library wishing to develop in tandem with the rest of the school needs to play a part in this strategic planning. In this way the library will be seen very much as part of the whole school and not as a satellite.

Ideas in the development plan can form a basis on which a dialogue can be opened between the library staff and stakeholders of the school. Priorities for the school may well be established as priorities for the library – more support for certain children, establishing a Homework Club, more reading for pleasure to raise literacy levels, greater emphasis on Speaking and Listening giving opportunity for an author visit or two and some stories on CD or DVD. Take a look at your school's development plan and see what openings it presents for your library before you start any serious budget planning.

The Head Teacher and the Governing Body

These stakeholders are the leaders of the school and not only steer it in pursuit of realising its aims and objectives and reaching its targets but they also hold the purse strings. They will only allocate a budget to those who work with them to raise standards and achievement.

- Be clear about what you want to do and why.
- Be accurate about costs.
- Make a clear and concise business case.

It can be useful to establish a 'special relationship' with a member of the governing body who will be able to champion the cause of the library and may be able to tap into streams of funding reserved for special projects.

Teaching Staff and Support Staff

The staff obviously influence how the library is used – or not, depending on what's on offer. Therefore it is important to meet their needs. Don't make assumptions, go and ask them what they would like to use in the library and develop collections and resources that will support their work in the classroom.

> 'It's important to know what's being taught and when. That way you can purchase the right books, do research, make displays that tie into the curriculum, and find good websites.'
> —Nikki Heath, *TES Magazine*, 2009

Pupils

Children will only use the library if they can find what they want within it. They won't come back if it does not contain anything that interests them. Therefore solicit their opinion regarding the types of resources and activities on offer. Remember that although you will need to buy some of the most popular items requested you do not have to buy everything they ask for!!

On occasions there may seem to be a conflict of interest. For example the literacy co-ordinator may not regard graphic novels as 'proper books' or can't see the value of story CDs and considers that they have no place in a library. However, if the children are asking for them this fact can be used to justify their place on the shelf. It is their library too! It is your decision if you run the library!

Parents/Guardians

Parents and guardians may also like to have their opinion included in the library's development plan. They may well be great supporters and advocates for library development. After all learning is a partnership between home and school.

Do they need any particular resources to support their children with their homework and to help develop reading for pleasure? Ask and you may be surprised by their response!

Making Your Case

Your development plan doesn't have to be an extensive piece of writing. An annual review, rather than report, which leans towards being a more formal document is a good starting point. You need to look at the current school development plan, the current library development plan and last year's library budget and development plan.

A suggested format is:

- A covering page including title, author and date.

- An introduction outlining the role of the library and its services.

- A brief summary of last year's activities, the budget and how it was spent. The budget information can be presented on a spreadsheet making it easy for the reader to digest. Too much information presented in a dense series of paragraphs may not even be read! – see the SLA publication *Practical Paperwork: Policy Making and Development Planning for the Primary School Library* (SLA, 2007).

This leads into plans for the future. These can be presented using a simple table listing your major initiatives for the year. Remember to link them to the school development plan. Consider how the library can help the school achieve its objectives. There is no point in developing an extensive Anglo-Saxon history collection if the subject is not part of the school's History curriculum, on the other hand it may well be important to update the poetry section or the fiction section for the 7 to 8-year-olds. The library needs to be responsive to the whole school community. Remember not only to include details of the initiative but also the name of the person responsible for the implementation of each, planned completion date, cost and whether any training will be necessary for library staff.

Description of whole school objective

Describe how the library will support this? _____

Who is responsible? _____

When will it be completed? _____

Is training required? _____

How much will it cost? _____

All this data can be pulled together to make representation to the school managers for next year's library budget.

The budget is likely to be allocated sometime at the beginning of the financial year. Ensure you are well prepared by making an early start.

If you make a bid for extra funding (which in fact shouldn't be necessary for your basic library funding) that is unsuccessful you will at least have alerted the Head Teacher and Governors to your needs and they may well be sympathetic if funds become available during the year or when it comes to allocating funds for next year.

Allocating the Library Budget

By the middle of the Summer Term (or the middle of the Autumn Term if you are an academy) you should know how much budget has been allocated to the library. It is now up to you to spend it wisely in accordance with your planning.

1. Allocating by Resource

A budget sheet will help ensure that all areas are adequately covered. If you use a spreadsheet you can make projections and then alter them and clearly see the effect of changing expenditure under each heading.

Main budget heading	Current amount	% of total
Fiction Replacement stock New stock	 £ £	
Picture books Replacement stock New stock	 £ £	
Non-fiction Replacement stock New stock	 £ £	
Reference	£	
ICT Hardware Software Consumables Subscriptions e.g. LMS Help	 £ £ £ £	
Newspapers, magazines and comics	£	
Office Stationery Equipment Reprographics Postage	 £ £ £ £	

Miscellaneous		
SLS subscription	£	
SLA subscription	£	
Repairs	£	
Professional development/training	£	
Furnishings and fittings	£	
Events/promotions	£	
Contingency fund	£	
TOTAL	£	

If you need to explain yourself further, the budget can be broken down so that school managers can see how these totals have been reached. For example:

Book stock	
Number of books divided by number of pupils i.e. books in the library stock per pupil	
Total stock required	
Stock level	
Shortfall	
Replacement stock required (usually 10% of total stock)	
Total cost (multiply average book price ❖ by number of replacement stock)	
Number of items required to bring stock up to recommended level	
Number of extra items required for stock development	
Annual budget maintenance level	
Stock development figures	
Total £	

❖ Average book price as given at SLA website:
www.sla.org.uk/advice-average-price.php (Members Only part of the website)

10% replacement may need some explanation to school managers as in some schools that is a considerable sum! Advise them as to why stock needs replacing – condition, age, currency, lost items. Books don't last forever, those with yellowing paper and missing pages will not be borrowed and therefore do little to assist in the raising of standards in literacy. Outdated information is unreliable and will not contribute to raising standards in teaching and learning! It maybe that 10% as a replacement figure is too high for your school, so come to an agreement with the Head Teacher as to the policy and clearly state the figures in documentation for others to read and understand. This figure may well take new SLS books into account and of course should include replacement/new stock that is put into classroom book corners.

2. Allocating the Funds Across the Curriculum

Funds can be allocated across the curriculum/subject areas as a result of specific resource requests to support teaching and learning by age range, especially for non-fiction books and ICT subject/topic specific materials.

A simple chart can illustrate which subject areas/topics are best supported by the library but much of the stock will have a cross curricular value. It can also be difficult to map how well each subject area uses the library, particularly if the library is not staffed or the resources that are used in the library are not recorded.

Remember to reserve some funds to spend on items for reading for pleasure and leisure. It's not all about work and passing exams!

Subject area	Library use	£ required for development planning	Provisional allocation of budget
English			
Maths			
Science			
Art			
Religious Education			
ICT			
Design and technology			
History			
Geography			
Music			
Others			

3. Allocation by numbers on roll

The budget can be allocated by the number on roll in a particular age group:

- Reception
- Key Stage 1
- Key Stage 2.

You can calculate the percentage of each group on roll and allocate funds accordingly.

	Number on roll	% of school	Provisional allocation of funding
Reception			£
Key Stage 1			£
Key Stage 2			£

4. Departments/Key Stage classes sharing costs

There is never enough money! Costs for larger, more expensive resources such as reference books, online resources, software or hardware can be shared with other departments/subject areas that have a vested interest in their use. You might like to approach one or more to spread the cost of purchasing, for example, an online encyclopaedia, which will be used by many subject areas across all age ranges.

In reality you will probably adopt a combination of approaches in order that the maximum amount of funding can be raised for the library.

5. Contingency funds

Remember to put 3% to 5% of your budget aside to cover unexpected costs such as:

- Unforeseen price rises
- Unexpected bills
- Breakages/urgent repairs/replacements.

I'm sure that it won't be difficult to spend these funds at the end of the financial year should you be fortunate enough to hang onto them!

The Annual Budget Cycle: A Summary

The Summer Term (Autumn Term for Academies)

This is the time of year when all your hard work comes to fruition. Previous consultation with the school community should ensure that your library is able to support teaching and learning with the relevant resources. You will be informed of your budget allocation and now is the time to:

- Allocate essential spending
- Balance your allocation against what you asked for and adjust your budget accordingly
- Allocate the remainder against other priorities
- Start placing orders for the next academic year or current year if you are an Academy.

Try not to spend all your budget allocation during this term but evenly throughout the academic year. However, ensure it is spent wisely! Conversely don't spend against next year's budget. If funds run low discuss the matter with your Line Manager/Head Teacher/School Managers so that the matter is addressed.

To ensure that the library's budget is spent efficiently and effectively it is wise to develop a cycle of key times to consult the school community regarding library expenditure and subsequently plan, order, monitor and evaluate spending.

This is probably the busiest term for academies as you will have new pupils to register and inductions to run.

The Autumn Term (Spring Term for Academies)

This is probably the busiest time for the library in LEA schools – new pupils to register, inductions for pupils and new staff to consider etc. As you settle into the term remember to:

- Continue ordering against your development plan
- Keep a check on expenditure
- Monitor and evaluate library use and keep notes in order that you can begin to plan next year's budget proposal.

Staff may not consider talking about their curricular needs with library staff and it is a good idea to begin discussions so that you establish priorities and requirements for the next academic year.

Try to be in a position to draft your development plan and bid by the end of the Autumn Term for LEA schools and the end of the Spring Term for academies.

The Spring Term
(Summer Term for Academies)

- Reflect upon and fine-tune the budget bid for next year.

- Be prepared! Often unexpected funding becomes available, especially at the end of the financial year. Carefully laid plans will ensure that you can quickly pull together a case and bid for it.

- Spend any small amounts remaining in your account including any petty cash. This might be a good time to treat some of the pupils by arranging for them to visit a local bookshop with you and choose some books.

- Ensure that you can account for all money including things like payments for lost books and photocopying just in case they are required for an audit.

Conclusion

All primary school libraries face considerable pressures on funding for stock and development necessitating a *'quality over quantity approach'*. As the SLA knows so well, primary school library coordinators continue to demonstrate innovative methods of facing stock shortages including using their SLS effectively, holding book fairs and including resources from book corners in the library stock. The SLA, Booktrust and Ofsted have all found that funding for school libraries varies markedly and all report that there is a direct link between well-funded libraries and effectiveness. However, gaps in resourcing are less significant overall than under-use or poor management.

Budget proposals are a key annual document that all library staff need to create and use as a working document. Budget discussion, creation and monitoring is cyclical, an ongoing process. Collaboration between teachers, teaching assistants and the people responsible for your library is essential to develop links between the library and the curriculum, in order to enrich learning and enable children to become readers for life and independent and confident users of information. Good luck with your budget planning and spending.

Case Study 1

Planning the Library Budget

Dean Close Preparatory School, Cheltenham

Rachel Sargeant BLib (Hons), MA, DMS, MCLIP
School Librarian, Dean Close Preparatory School

Dean Close Preparatory School (DCPS) is an independent school in Cheltenham, Gloucestershire, with approximately 300 pupils, including 70 boarders.

DCPS comes under the umbrella of the Dean Close Foundation. This comprises the prep, a pre-prep and Dean Close School (the senior school in Cheltenham) as well as St John's on the Hill prep, pre-prep and nurseries in Chepstow.

At DCPS, the age range is 7 to 13 years. There are three mixed ability classes in the year groups 3 to 6. Classes are streamed in Years 7 and 8. Class sizes are small, not more than 20 pupils per class. At the end of Year 8, DCPS pupils take their Common Entrance exam to go onto their senior school of choice. Most go on to Dean Close School.

The Dean Close Foundation operates one Bursary [finance department] based in the senior school. Although DCPS is largely autonomous with its own senior management team and I report to the Deputy Head Academic, all of us apply to the Bursary for our budgets.

Background to DCPS Library

I was appointed to the post of School Librarian in January 2015. The School had not had a professional librarian for some time and wanted someone to oversee the move to a new library. Redundant office accommodation had become available and presented the opportunity to create a larger, brighter and more central site for the library. Dean Close Estates Team carried out the conversion and I designed the new library. This project was an unplanned opportunity without a budget. We were able to undertake the work because of the resources and expertise of the Dean Close Foundation. The Bursary accepted my case that we should buy shelving from a specialist library supplier (not easy when we had no budget).

The Library is open at break and at lunchtime for pupils to read, borrow books, do research or listen to audiobooks. I am on duty during this time to supervise the children (up to 55 pupils) and to help with research and book choices. I am also in the Library from 8am for pupils or parents seeking advice or wishing to return/borrow books.

Teachers book lesson time in the Library for their pupils to research topics or for quiet reading. Some teachers ask me to prepare and support these lessons, others prefer to run the lessons themselves.

I run a series of subject-specific research lessons and hold reading workshops, and every class has an induction session at the start of the year. We also use the Library for author visits etc.

The current stock comprises the following sections: Fiction (approx. Years 4–6); Young Fiction (approx. Years 3–4); Young Adult (Years 7–8); Picture Books; Graphic Novels; Browser Non-fiction; Non-fiction; Reference; Audiobooks.

There are various types of seating and two computers for schoolwork and for pupils to check emails.

The Budgeting Process

The process starts in late November when I complete a budget bid spreadsheet, detailing the items of spend I require for the Library for the following academic year (September to August). The spreadsheet has two parts: the recurring bid for routine items that I need year on year; and the non-recurring bid for one-off items costing more than £250.

A draft budget for the whole school is presented to the Finance and General Purpose Committee and then to the Board of Trustees for approval in the Lent [Spring] term. It is subsequently updated to take account of changes in pupil numbers, payroll and other adjustments, and the final budget is presented for approval in the Trinity [Summer] term. I am notified of my budget allocation at the end of August.

The recurring budget bid can end up with one of three outcomes: approved; approved but with a general reduction requiring me to adjust spending in all categories; or approved except for specific items which have been removed from the budget. The non-recurring budget may be completely declined.

The allocated budget can only be spent on items that have been approved. I must seek permission in advance if I find during the year that certain items are not needed and I wish to spend funds on other areas. Some organisations penalise budget holders who underspend. However, Dean Close sensibly sees that an underspend can assist the School's overall surplus and cash flow position.

Library Budget Bid

The recurring budget bid template for academic budgets is arranged, understandably, for teaching departments. It is adapted for the Library. There are three columns: Category, Description and Cost. The first two columns of my bid for the coming year are printed below. (At the time of writing, this bid has not yet been approved.)

Category	Description
General	First News – Children's newspaper subscription
	How It Works Magazine – annual subscription
	Phoenix Comic – term-time subscription
	SLA Professional Development Publications
Textbooks	Fiction: Yr 3-4, continue updating process for fiction – 50
	Fiction: Yr 5-6, continue updating process for fiction – 70
	Fiction: Yr 7-8, continue updating process for fiction – 50
	Non-fiction: continue updating process for non-fiction – 50
	Reference Books: language dictionaries and atlases – £100
	Browser books and graphic novels – 60
Equipment/Materials	Audio books: continue to update – 8
	Beanbags – 2
	Library stationery, e.g. spine labels, date labels
	Display items

The Deputy Head Academic holds a budget for staff training which enables me to attend professional development courses without having to use Library funds. IT costs are currently met by another department.

It is very clear from this bid that I aim to spend considerably more on fiction than on non-fiction. This is part of my long-term strategy to improve fiction provision and encourage reading for pleasure. I intend to review the non-fiction in the future, but I know I cannot do everything at once so I have prioritised fiction and 'browser' non-fiction.

The reasons for that decision are:

■ The move to the new site provided the opportunity to rearrange and weed the stock. The large non-fiction collection was in reasonable, up-to-date condition thanks to the attention of the Head of English and the library adviser from Gloucestershire Schools Library Service. It was only necessary to carry out a light weed and to categorise the subject areas. The introduction of colour-coded subject categories while retaining the Dewey numbers has led to a more child-friendly and better used collection.

■ Teachers often request non-fiction topic boxes, e.g. twenty books on Greek myths, the Aztecs, habitats, food and digestion etc to have in their classrooms for the six-week duration of the topic. Because the teachers in each year group work closely together, they are able to share each topic box. This makes demand manageable for the Library. It is an area I intend to review in the year after next, once the more pressing need to improve the fiction has been addressed.

■ The fiction stock needed an overhaul. It has so far taken 18 months to update the stock. I anticipate it taking another year. Old, unloved stock had taken up space on the shelves and brought down the appeal of the whole collection. It is noticeable that, as old stock is removed, pupils start to see the new stock more clearly and read it.

■ In the old library there was an embarrassingly tatty collection of old copies of the *Guinness World Records*. They had broken spines and ripped pages and were propped up on unsuitable metal shelving. The children swarmed to that eyesore every break and lunchtime. They couldn't get enough of these sad excuses for library books. It was clear that I needed to address that stock area urgently. I felt that it could not wait until the next budget application and I obtained permission to spend some of my book fund on an attractive browser box. I also spent fiction funds on multiple copies of the new *Guinness World Records* and other similar fact/browser books. The Library had very few graphic novels although these were also popular so I made a note to bid for graphic novels in the next budget round.

One year later, I have established attractive and hugely popular collections of browser books and graphic novels. It is quite noticeable that behaviour has improved at break and lunchtime now that pupils have something light and quick to read during their rest times between lessons. My current budget bid reflects the need to consolidate these new collections.

This year I experimented with having small, circulating collections of challenging and experimental novels in the younger-age classrooms. I changed the collections every month and gave a five-minute pitch to classes to promote individual titles. This worked well despite some of the stock in the collections being already familiar to the pupils. I have bid this year to spend more on Year 5/6 fiction to develop this project.

My non-recurring budget bid is the same as my previous year's declined bid for new island shelving for fiction. The Bursar felt that the Library did very well out of the refurbishment with the supply of excellent wall shelving for non-fiction and Young Adult, and so the Library is not a priority for more shelving. I keep on asking because I know what a difference it will make to the children's interest in the fiction stock on display.

Tips for Making a Budget Bid

■ Come up with a baseline budget based on the SLA recommendation of renewing 10% of stock per year. This needs to be a detailed exercise, looking at each category of stock separately. So, for example, you have 1,000 junior fiction novels. The average cost of a paperback novel for that age group, taking into account suppliers' discounts and processing costs is £6. Therefore, you need to bid for £600 to maintain your fiction section. Repeat this for all categories of stock, and don't forget to add on other day-to-day running costs like SLA membership, magazine subscriptions and stationery.

■ A baseline budget calculation can be particularly helpful if you are new in post. You can compare it with what has been allocated in previous years. If there has been significant long-term underfunding, it's worth using your calculations to challenge this.

■ Before you submit your budget, decide whether you want to maintain existing stock levels. Does current provision meet the needs of your long-term strategy for the library? Do some sections need expanding while others could be contracted? What do you want your stock, and your budget, to achieve? Adjust your baseline bid accordingly.

- Observe how your library is being used. Who is in there reading? What are they reading? Know what's popular and where there is unfulfilled demand. How is inadequate furniture or other equipment affecting behaviour or interest in reading? Ask pupils for their views. Analyse loan statistics.

- Observe reading/research throughout the school and decide how this might affect library purchasing. Ask teachers how they use books in the classroom, and how you can support this. The Library is there to complement classroom provision, not duplicate it.

- Establish relationships with all teaching departments and encourage them to express their library needs. You don't want to waste money on curriculum resources if they are not right for your school.

- Remember that you don't have to buy everything a teacher asks for. If, in your professional judgement, it is not something the library should stock, explain your decision.

- Have a long-term Library Development plan that is approved by the senior management team and complements the School Development plan. Your spending should be in support of this plan.

- Be realistic, don't ask for more funds than you really need. Be clear on what is essential and what is desirable. Present yourself as a credible manager for your school.

- Don't spend money just because you have it in your budget. Clogging up bookshelves with new but unwanted novels will not increase library usage or turn more pupils into keen readers. Instead, request to spend spare funds in a different way and justify your request.

- Add to a wish list throughout the year as things occur to you and as you observe library use. Compare this with your development plan when it is time to write your next bid.

- Shop around for the most reliable suppliers and factor in the cost of processing stock. It is probably more cost-effective to pay a few pence for the supplier to jacket and label each book than for you to spend your library/teaching time sitting in an office doing it.

- Try to spend your budget steadily throughout the year and expect the unexpected. I had to request budget changes to deal with a collapsed, beyond repair bookcase and a pile of 400 books.

- Keep accurate records of your spending. You may need to query the figures that your finance department has kept, or you may be asked to account for actual expenditure in a particular stock category.

- Evaluate income generation methods to boost your budget, such as distributing book club catalogues or holding book fairs. If they are value for money and encourage pupils to read, get involved. Alternatively, investigate an arrangement with a local bookshop.

- Look at ways of saving the school money. For example, it might be cheaper and more accessible to stock magazines in the library rather than in teaching departments. Remember that you are part of the whole school team.

Case Study 2

Planning the School Library Budget
Globe Primary School

Lucy Chambers BA Hons, M.Inf.Sci, MCLIP

Primary School Librarian, Tower Hamlets Schools Library Services

---

Introduction

I am part of a team of peripatetic primary school librarians. I run several libraries from 3.5 hours to 7 hours a week.

In some schools I remain librarian for one year (minimum contract) and then hand over to a member of school staff, in others I stay for several years.

I have a vision of the development of my libraries over time and a library policy document. What I achieve depends on the working relationship I have with the school, budget and other factors, such as number of hours employed there. Time is also a factor of course: generally the more hours I work in the school per week, the more projects I can undertake, thus improving the impact I can have.

I aim to spend equal time on library administration, resource promotion (this includes work with staff and children) and strategic management. In some schools I work beyond the library, for example running literacy audits across the school, offering INSETs to staff, looking after classroom collections and advising on curriculum texts.

My main roles are to develop well-resourced, organised and effective libraries, to promote reading for pleasure, to teach information skills, and to develop children's creativity and lifelong learning skills through reading and related activities.

Background to the Schools Library Services (SLS)

The SLS is a subscription-financed organisation within London Borough of Tower Hamlets. Primary and secondary schools in Tower Hamlets and neighbouring boroughs buy in to it annually. There are various levels of service on offer, such as topic resource loans for teachers, joint subscriptions to online tools, a package of author visits, participation in SLS-organised events and the option for primary schools to hire a professional librarian from 3.5 hours a week to full-time. There are different pricing packages depending on the options chosen by schools.

Background to Globe Primary School

Globe Primary School is a state school in London Borough of Tower Hamlets, a socially deprived area. It is above average in size with 363 pupils, with 59.7% eligible for Pupil Premium (all figures from 2014 OFSTED Dashboard) and a very high proportion of its pupils speak English as an additional language. The majority of pupils are of Bangladeshi heritage, with African and White British heritage the next largest groups. 16.3% have a school action plan or are SEN, which puts the school in the highest national percentile.

The significance of the high level of social deprivation and high SEN levels of the school demographic is that Tower Hamlets schools have until now had generous funding relative to state schools elsewhere. With the current proposed Government changes to the school funding formula this is set to change, with money being channelled from London schools to schools nationally. In addition, the school demographic is changing as property prices rise locally, with fewer children being eligible for Pupil Premium funding. This is in addition to the general increases in National Insurance and teachers' pay. These political changes are having a major impact on school budgets in inner London. In these circumstances, some schools are reluctantly cutting their subscriptions to the SLS and to this innovative and very successful programme we have of supplying professional librarians to schools.

Budgets

I have been librarian here since April 2006 and currently work seven hours a week.

The library was furnished before I arrived. I was responsible for selecting, cataloguing and processing the stock and establishing the library at the centre of school life. The school received a grant of £20,000 from a charitable trust to cover shelving and stock and put in an additional c.£8,000 from school reserves, as well as £1,000 for a team of SLS librarians to weed, classify, catalogue and label the new books and integrate it with the old stock.

The library annual budget has gradually reduced over the years.

Years	Amount
2007 to 2009	£2000
2010 to 2014	£1000
2015 to 2017	No specified amount: told to only buy essentials
The future	Probably even less

I spend the budget carefully and am always looking for value for money. I usually order online via a book supplier that gives a good discount and get all books jacketed and labelled by them according to my instructions. They send lists of the chosen titles for me to classify. I also buy book collections from remainder booksellers, which are usually much cheaper but don't include servicing, which takes time. If I am buying non-fiction I may go direct to specialist publishers who often offer very good discounts (but no servicing).

However for spending large sums (£1,000+) I visit a book supplier with a showroom, even though the discount is much less, as I then have the opportunity to choose from a wider age-specific selection. Again, I ask the book supplier to process the books as above. Time = money.

Annual budget requests

I submit a budget request annually, as all curriculum subject leads do. I base my request on the Booktrust recommended level of 13 books per child per year at the average cost of a book, 10% loss and damage replacement, my projects, what I applied for the previous year, general stock renewal plans, my current subscriptions and school requirements.

I receive the new budget amount in April and have to spend it by the following February. This allows the Bursar a few weeks to receive and pay invoices before the end of the financial year. I aim to spend an equal amount each term.

School plans

The library is not usually on the School Improvement Plan (S.I.P.), as OFSTED does not usually visit or make comment, but my work is often mentioned when teachers discuss working towards literacy targets. I have regular meetings with the Literacy Coordinator/Deputy Head to discuss targets and how I can be involved and will reflect school needs on my budget request when possible. I need to ensure the library is recognised as essential to the school.

Sample library budget request

Item	Amount requested	Impact on school
Book requests/replacement stock/ curriculum stock	£1000	Booktrust recommended levels to maintain effective library
Magazine/newspaper subscriptions	£200	*Develop range of reading material for whole school:* Current titles read regularly by KS1 and 2
Library stationery	£100	Essential to maintain stock condition and longevity
SLS events: Book Award shortlist x 3	£150	*Gifted and Talented; debating skills; aspirational reading; empathy reading performance skills:* Running Book Award club for 20 high-level readers in Years 5 and 6
Book Award shortlists: Greenaway/Royal Soc. Science books/ SLA Information Book Award	£150	*Develop visual literacy skills; debating skills; comparison skills; study non-fiction books:* to be shared by Chatterbooks Club and classes Years 2 to 6
New curriculum books (School Improvement Plan)	£1000	*Improve library stock for whole school to support the new curriculum topics*
Guided readers, short novels (SIP)	£300	*Clubs for targeted groups of children not reading at home:* Year 4

Budget nuances

There are different levels of budget for different purposes. You need a start-up budget for setting up or re-establishing the library, then annual amounts to spend on resources. It is often easier to get the former than the latter. All Heads love one-off capital projects. To counter this approach, I inform the Head of projects from external bodies relevant to literacy and reading in general and try and tag on a library angle, thus generating new resources and whole school impact.

Some examples:

- **'No Outsiders' project**: the school took part in this to ensure the availability of books about LGBT, special needs and disabilities. The Head asked me to select and order suitable level books for every class from the reading list the trainer supplied. I successfully requested that I also had copies of all the chosen books in the library.

- **New curriculum topics**: Each time the school has changed curriculum topics I have been asked to select books for topic boxes. What happens to the books from the previous curriculum? They are given to the library. If they are still current and relevant, I add them to stock.

- **Author visits**: The Head is always happy for me to buy several copies of all their books for the library and relevant classes, either from the library or literacy budget and also borrow copies from the SLS for display on the day. I report on the success of the author visit, quoting the loan figures for the author's books, sales and any positive comments children make.

- **Humanities Education Centre projects**: HEC is part of the SLS and works on Citizenship and Development Education projects with schools using funding from grants. I promote these projects to schools and if I find out one has been taken up, I try and ensure some library involvement

- **Special literary events**: We have run Harry Potter Night celebrations since 2014, which enable me not only to sell the books to parents but also to obtain several copies of the new edition for the library.

Other school budgets for library-related items or librarian-generated projects

Some regular costs related to running the library always come from other budgets:

- Junior Librarian computer system help desk, upgrades and annual subscription: IT budget

- The school subscription to the SLS and fees payable for hiring me: school core funding

- SLS events related to Literacy and run by teachers in class, such as the Creative Writing Competition and the Poetry Slam: Literacy budget

- Author visits: Literacy budget, even though I usually run them

- Book Week/after-school family reading events: dedicated budget
  An example of this was **Fathers' Story Week**:
    the Home/School Officer and I worked together on this and ran the following activities: visiting storyteller across the school for a day, two film nights, art competition with prizes, family assembly, fathers sharing stories in class,

father/school team cricket match and family party including display of art work created. The ideas and basic resources came from a free website and we held three planning meetings. The only costs other than staff time were £300 for the storyteller and £30 for the prizes, both of which were covered by the project budget.

- Books for classroom collections: Literacy budget
- Teacher resources for topic boxes: Literacy budget
- Requests from Head: Head's budget or Literacy budget

  An example of this was **Class collections**:

  the Head asked me to select and order up to 20 non-fiction and mixed genre books for each new main curriculum topic for every class. This was very expensive and came out of the Literacy budget over two years.

Finding out about these budgets is easier if you are on good terms with the Bursar and various subject coordinators. I either negotiate these items by discussion or am asked by the Head or Deputy to undertake the project. I don't necessarily include them in my annual budget request.

Accountability and record keeping

I keep a spreadsheet of all library orders and which budget they have come from. I produce a library impact report for the Head, Literacy Coordinator, SMT and governors every term, including the library budget spending and use made of the SLS and value of the resources borrowed. This latter figure looks impressive, especially compared to the size of the library budget.

What happens if the library budget is inadequate?

Firstly, I meet the Head and Literacy Coordinator to discuss my aims for the year and negotiate possible solutions.

The ideal scenario is to receive funds so that I can choose the books needed, but this is not always possible. Some ideas are below:

- **SLS**: I encourage staff to borrow resources for their class topics every term and borrow books for the library and class collections on a regular basis. This is a great way of having a regular turnover of new books, as they can be changed every term for a new selection.

- **Targeted groups**: Read the professional education press to get an idea of what groups need encouraging in education and plan a project to work with them in the school.

  For example, I targeted Pupil Premium children who had no literacy support at home. My budget request included a sum to cover suitable resources for this. I produced two reports demonstrating how the sessions and resources improved their attainment.

- **Donations**: I accept 'as new' book donations from parents, but say that if they are not suitable I will donate them to school sales; I also ask contacts in wealthier London boroughs for donations of children's books.

- **New books**: I apply to publishers for offers of free copies of newly published or pre-publication proofs. Some publishers send several copies for review, others send individual titles. I also collect free books from conferences, meetings and courses I attend. It all helps.

- **Wishlist**: I keep a wish list in case of small amounts of money available from other budgets at the end of the financial year. By keeping good contacts with book suppliers I can spend such sums speedily on targeted resources.

- **Scholastic Book Fairs**: hold these regularly in school and collect the profit in free books; ask parents to buy a book for the school when buying a book for their child.

- **Websites**: Some book websites generate funds or books for libraries.

- **Fundraising**: not easy in Tower Hamlets schools but a possible approach.

- **Reading Partners/local firms**: ask for help with fundraising or for an amount for a specific project. Probably best done through the school.

- **Grants**: I apply for grants for specific projects. For example, I received £500 from a small trust fund for subscriptions to magazines for classrooms. Some of my other schools have received quite generous grants for books from the Foyle Foundation.

Conclusion

Globe Primary School is undergoing major budget cuts at present. As Librarian, I need to be resourceful in order to maintain and preferably develop the library and the range of activities that I provide for the school. I need to advocate for librarians more than ever and demonstrate the impact of my work on the pupils' educational attainment both while they are at primary school and in the future.

Appendix 1

A sample of primary school library budgets from a range of English schools

Compiled by Geoff Dubber

Having just read a publication about primary school library budgeting the one thing that all readers will ponder is the size of the library budget in other schools… to compare with their own.

In the early Autumn of 2016 a dozen friends/colleagues at random were invited to supply budget information – all guaranteed anonymity as data of this nature is often seen as sensitive by schools, although all Head Teachers should be able to explain/justify the annual totals provided to anyone who asks.

Some didn't reply at all and one worked across a range of schools.

Here is the information received.

General comments from one primary school librarian working in the south of England

I work across a group of schools. Most of my schools are tightening their belts due to the proposed new funding formula, which is threatened to remove funding from our area to distribute it more fairly nationally. I feel that my job is constantly at risk. Two schools stopped employing me for financial reasons. Their libraries are now run by full-time teachers. Some schools have better reserves or income and there has been no change to my budget, with one being very generous. One school is paying for the Accelerated Reader books from School Improvement money.

For schools with low budget I apply for grants, and think up projects which will generate books or provide library funding from other budgets. I also try and bring money, authors, activities and events into the school, so that the Head will see that my presence is essential and that the library is worth funding. These tactics don't always work or they take a long time, but I keep on trying!

In one school this year I suggested that four classes read and discuss the Greenaway shortlist, so I bought four sets of the list from the Literacy budget. These now reside in the library. I also borrow crates of new fiction from the local SLS for the library and encourage all staff to borrow their quota each term. I would ask parents for book donations, but the demographic here is very mixed, with many unemployed parents and 40% or so Pupil Premium children, so fundraising is very poor. I encourage the schools to hold regular Scholastic Bookfairs so that the profit in books can be used in the library. I complete a budget bid every February itemising what I intend to spend it on and usually request c. £2,000 but, as you can see from the varied figures, the Heads don't take much notice!

School & Type of school	Number on Roll	15/16 budget	% rise or fall from 14/15	Notes and comments from schools
School 1 **State – Primary** **3 – 11 age range** Librarian here 1 day a week; Have been here several years.	360+	None set, but see notes	£1000, down from £2350 in 13/14	Head said 'spend what you need.' But she didn't veto anything I gave her to sign so I decided I 'needed' £1000. I also bought teacher and literacy resources using the Literacy budget, which was also much curtailed from the previous year to a similar 'needs only' basis. In previous years the Literacy budget was £12,000 a year. 16/17: No budget again. Head is being stricter and scrutinising my orders more, so I buy fiction secondhand, apply for free samples (successfully), ask for donations and tout for any free author visits. Am applying for grants.
School 2 **State Primary** **3 – 11 age range** Librarian: was 3.5 hours a week, but now no longer employed. Was there 6 years, for 4 of them for 1 day a week.	220+	£500	£500	This was supplemented in 15/16 by a £5000 grant from Foyle Foundation. Of the grant, half was spent on library books, allowing me to update the collection and duplicate popular titles as well as buying resources for the new curriculum. The rest was spent by the Lit Coordinator on guided readers, Accelerated Reader books and levelled readers.
School 3 **State Primary** **3 – 11 age range** Librarian: was employed 1 day a week, but has now left; I was there for 2 years, 1 year with no library!	470+	In the school's Literacy budget – no separate library budget	None. See notes	In 14/15 I set up a small library and was given £2000 to buy basic stock and £2000 for shelving from Finnmade. Book award shortlists and other resources needed for clubs. Author visits etc were funded from the Literacy budget.

			Comments
School 4 **State Primary** **3 – 11 age range** Librarian: 1 day a week from Sept 2015	320+	Capital sum and grant spent. See comments.	n/a	This school is gradually expanding from 1-form entry to a 3-form entry school. New library opened January 2016. Capital sum spent on library furniture: £7000; books £8000, plus a grant of £7000 from Foyle Foundation. Budget 2016/17 is a whopping £8000, plus an additional £5000 to spend on Accelerated Reader books, as the school is starting this in Jan 2017 for Years 5 and 6.
School 5 **State Primary** **3 – 11 age range** Librarian: 3.5 hours a week. I started 2015, but they had previously employed a librarian for 9 years.	470+	£1500	£1500	Budget of £1500 has been maintained for several years. The library heavily used and in need of substantial input, so I am currently applying for grants.
School 6 **State Primary** **3 – 11 age range** Librarian: 3.5 hours a week from April 2015	220+	None, but capital sum from grant spent. See notes.	£1000	From April 2015, I weeded and restocked the library with a grant of £10,000 from Canary Wharf Group. I am the first librarian the school has had, starting in April 2015. Previously the Head applied for a grant every 10 years and restocked library; I persuaded her to allocate money every year to maintain the stock and replenish gradually. Author/theatre visits, literacy resources and class collections come from Literacy budget.
School 7 **Independent Prep School** **3 – 11 age range** In S.E. England	n/a	n/a	n/a	No library statistics. Sorry.

School	Population			Notes
School 8 Independent **Prep School.** South of England		£4,200	£4,200	The library budget is supplemented by commission from our annual book fair (approx £300). Also the annual cost of Junior Librarian net is covered by the whole school IT budget. The library budget does however contribute to the annual cost of our Accelerated Reader programme, the library share is approx £750.
School 9 **State Junior (Academy status)** **7 – 11 age range** N. W. England	200+	n/a	n/a	Really sorry that I cannot answer this question! There is no formal library budget. I ask for resources as I need them and the head either says yes or no. I wonder if that's the same case in many primary schools?!
School 10 **International School** in S.E.England	n/a	£6980 A fall of 2.7% on the previous year	n/a	It is a very generous budget and my budget fluctuates depending on the number of pupils on the school roll. So there are more pupils this year and my budget is higher.
School 11 **State Primary** **4 – 11 age range** Eastern England	210+ 650+	£200 left once the MLS help desk is paid for	n/a	My budget has been in a parlous state for the last few years. I am no longer the budget holder – this is the responsibility of the teacher who is subject leader for the library and my line manager [the assistant head who is also English leader]. Out of my £200 I ensure that the SLA membership is paid, with the rest going on covering materials, some Carel Press purchases and other necessaries – as you can imagine hardly anything is spent on books! I buy stock using commission from book fairs such as Travelling Books and Scholastic Books, hold sales of retired library books and donate review copies that I receive. The school does subscribe to our SLS (now called Literacy, Books and Reading Team for Schools] which costs around £3,000 and is essential – we use them for topic box loans [1 per class per term] plus stock to supplement the library collection – this comes out of the ESS budget.

Appendix 2

Table: Approximate Budgets by School Size

School Size (Range)	Library Budget £								Base (No.)
	Up to 250	251 – 500	501 – 1000	1001 – 1500	1501 – 2000	2001 – 2500	2501 – 3000	3001 or more	
50 or less	1	1	2	0	0	0	0	0	4
51-100	2	3	4	1	0	0	0	1	11
101-150	1	3	0	1	2	0	0	2	9
151-200	0	3	3	4	3	0	1	2	16
201-250	0	3	5	1	2	0	2	7	20
251-300	0	1	3	0	0	0	0	0	4
301-350	0	0	1	2	2	0	0	4	9
351-400	0	2	2	0	0	1	0	2	7
401-450	0	1	0	1	0	0	0	1	3
451 or more	0	1	0	1	0	0	1	4	7

Source: Booktrust – *Library Books in Schools. Spending and Provision in Primary and Secondary Schools in England.* 2007. http://booktrustadmin.kentlyons.com/downloads/publicfinance.pdf

Further References

CILIP/SLA/ASCEL: *Primary School Guidelines* (2016). Includes a section about budgeting: http://primaryschoollibraryguidelines.org.uk/policyAndPlanning/budgets

Dubber, Geoff & Dring, Sally. *Careful with Cash: Managing the Secondary School Library Budget*. School Library Association, 2012.

Duncan, Sally. *Making a Start with your Primary School Library*. School Library Association, 2010.

The Foyle Foundation provides funding for school libraries. To complete an application form see http://www.foylefoundation.org.uk/how-to-apply/state-schools.php

Greenwood, Helen, Creaser, Claire & Maynard, Sally. *Successful Primary School Libraries: Case Studies of Good Practice*. Loughborough University, 2008. Available at: http://www.lboro.ac.uk/microsites/infosci/lisu/downloads/successful-prim-sch-libs.pdf

Harrison, Kay & Adams, Tricia. *Practical Paperwork: Policy Making and Development Planning for the Primary School Library*. School Library Association, 2007.

IFLA. *IFLA School Library Guidelines* (2nd Ed, June 2015): Available at: http://www.ifla.org/files/assets/school-libraries-resource-centers/publications/ifla-school-library-guidelines.pdf

Lemaire, Kathy & Duncan, Sally. *Everything in its Place: Managing Electronic and Physical Resources in the School Library*. School Library Association, 2017.

National Library of New Zealand. *Your school library budget*. Available at: http://schools.natlib.govt.nz/school-libraries/collection-development/your-school-library-budget

Ofsted, 2006. *Good school libraries: Making a difference to learning*. Available at: http://dera.ioe.ac.uk/5792/

Rowan, Tanya. *Library Books in Schools: Spending and provision in primary and secondary schools in England*. BookTrust, 2007. Available at: http://s3.amazonaws.com/zanran_storage/booktrustadmin.kentlyons.com/ContentPages/2491899457.pdf

School Library Association. *School Libraries in 2012 – the SLA Survey*. Available at: http://www.sla.org.uk/sla-survey-2012.php

Scott, Elspeth, Duncan, Sally and Dubber, Geoff. *Quality and Impact: Measuring the Performance of your School Library*. School Library Association, 2011.